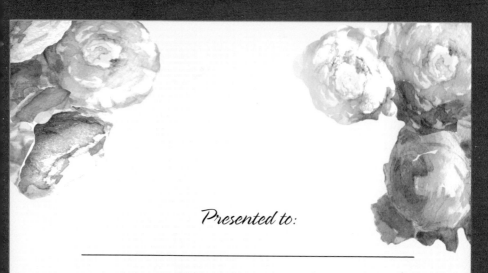

Presented to:

_____

Presented by:

_____

Date:

_____

Gifts
from my
Heart

Inspirational Thoughts, Insights, & Reflections

THE
POPULAR
G R O U P
New York, New York

Gifts from My Heart
ISBN 1-59027-047-9

Copyright © 2002 by GRQ Ink, Inc.
1948 Green Hills Blvd.
Franklin, Tennessee 37067

Published by **Popular Publishing Company, LLC**
3 Park Avenue
New York, New York 10016

Developed by GRQ Ink, Inc.
Cover and text design by Whisner Design Group, Tulsa, Oklahoma
Illustrations by Stephen Gilpin, Tulsa, Oklahoma
Text written by Harriet E. Crosby

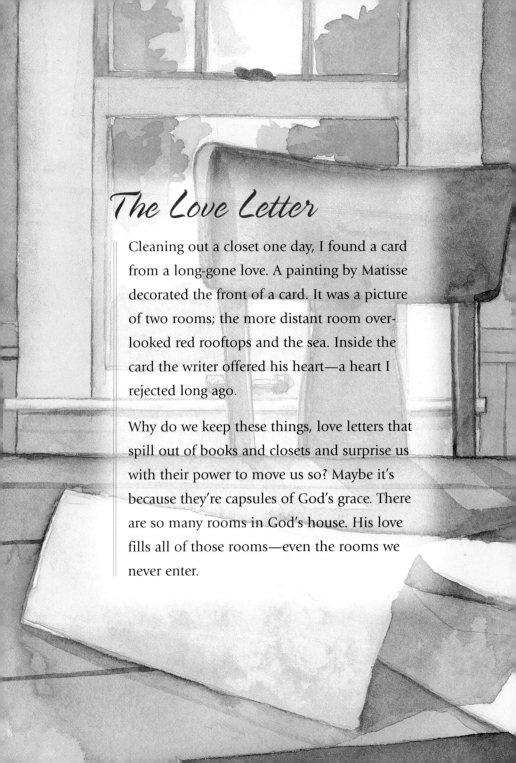

The Love Letter

Cleaning out a closet one day, I found a card from a long-gone love. A painting by Matisse decorated the front of a card. It was a picture of two rooms; the more distant room overlooked red rooftops and the sea. Inside the card the writer offered his heart—a heart I rejected long ago.

Why do we keep these things, love letters that spill out of books and closets and surprise us with their power to move us so? Maybe it's because they're capsules of God's grace. There are so many rooms in God's house. His love fills all of those rooms—even the rooms we never enter.

"In My Father's house are many mansions;
if it were *not* so,
I would have told you. I go to
prepare a place for you."

JOHN 14:2 NKJV

Thank you, O God, for love lost
and for love found.

Amen.

The Wedding Photograph

It's Florida in 1912. My grandmother is wearing a high-waisted white dress and has a serene expression on her face. She stands slightly behind my grandfather, who wears a suit, no tie, and a straw boater. Granny is solemn; Papa is smiling. It is their wedding day. They do not yet know the children they will bear. They do not yet know World War I and the Great Depression. The promises they made that day will sustain them through many hard times.

Similarly, God's promises unite us in love, joy, and hope. Through tragedy, hardship, and loss, He promises His undying love. He promises to be with us. We have His peace.

"*Peace I leave with you; my peace I give to you. I do not give to you as the world gives. Do not let your hearts be troubled, and do not let them be afraid.*"

JOHN 14:27 NRSV

Your promise of peace holds us together in love, O God.

Amen.

Barbie Love

My Barbie is thirty-seven years old. She stands stiffly on a bookshelf in my study, and she is still stunning. Her titian hair is styled in a perfect 1963 bubble. She is dressed in a bright red, hand-knitted sweater and skirt ensemble with tiny white buttons, a string of pearls, and brown stiletto sandals.

I'll never forget the afternoon, years ago, when Mom reunited me with Barbie and three big boxes filled with Mom's handmade Barbie clothes. We spent all afternoon trying those Jackie Kennedy–style clothes on Barbie and remembering our lives together when Mom made each piece. Now when I see Barbie dressed in clothes so lovingly made, I hear Mom say from Heaven, "I love you."

*And now these three remain:
faith, hope and love. But the
greatest of these is love.*

1 CORINTHIANS 13:13 NIV

—m—

O God, I thank You for my
mother's love, then—and now.
Amen.

Tell Me Again

My study is filled with books. A few of the books have been read and reread over the years. When I reread them, these books bring back memories of the first reading. I experience the same feelings of wonder I had when I was a little girl.

The Bible is one of my best friends. One edition is so dog-eared and worn from countless readings that I have to handle it gently to keep it from falling apart. My Bible reminds me of God, my first Love. It awakens in me the feelings of wonder and awe I experienced when I first believed as a young woman—such a precious gift! I ponder each word in my heart, as my Bible tells me again how much God loves me.

Remember my words with your whole being. Write them down and tie them to your hands as a sign; tie them on your foreheads to remind you.

DEUTERONOMY 11:18 NCV

Thank You, O God, for living in my memory and reminding me that You are my first Love.

Amen.

Keepsakes

In my living room is a glass case filled with my mother's crystal stemware. My father brought the stemware back from one of his tours of duty in the Navy in 1960. Each glass is etched with a delicate pattern of billowing wheat. The lovely crystal is from a glamorous era, when formal cocktail parties were the rage. There must be over a hundred glasses in the set—a glass for every conceivable kind of drink.

Why do I keep Mom's stemware? The glasses twinkle in their case, and they remind me of my mother as a lovely young woman. How I wish she were here now! But the stemware also reminds me that she is with God—and as young and lovely as ever.

If I'm sleepless at midnight,
I spend the hours
in grateful reflection.

Psalm 63:6 The Message

This keepsake, O Lord, reminds me
that You hold those I love in the palm
of Your hand. Thank You.
Amen.

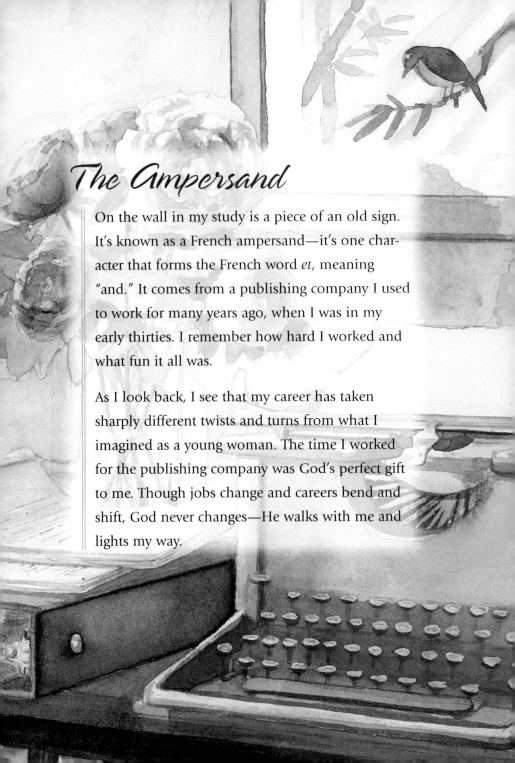

The Ampersand

On the wall in my study is a piece of an old sign. It's known as a French ampersand—it's one character that forms the French word *et*, meaning "and." It comes from a publishing company I used to work for many years ago, when I was in my early thirties. I remember how hard I worked and what fun it all was.

As I look back, I see that my career has taken sharply different twists and turns from what I imagined as a young woman. The time I worked for the publishing company was God's perfect gift to me. Though jobs change and careers bend and shift, God never changes—He walks with me and lights my way.

Every good and perfect gift is from above,
coming down from the Father of the heavenly
lights, who does not change
like shifting shadows.

JAMES 1:17 NIV

Lord, things didn't turn out the way I
thought they would, but the gift of Your
love always lights my path. Thank You.
Amen.

The Power of Place

Recently I visited my alma mater, the University of California at Berkeley. I hadn't been on campus for twenty-five years. As I walked through Sather Gate, the university's entrance, I was overcome by the power of this place to evoke memories. I remembered as a student feeling that I had the world by the tail, that the future was mine and very bright.

Standing in the redwood grove with my memories, I felt God's presence. God had given me the gift of an education and a lifelong love of books and learning—a gift that has brought me many successes and has sustained me through many defeats. I stood humbly on that holy ground before God who had brought me so very far.

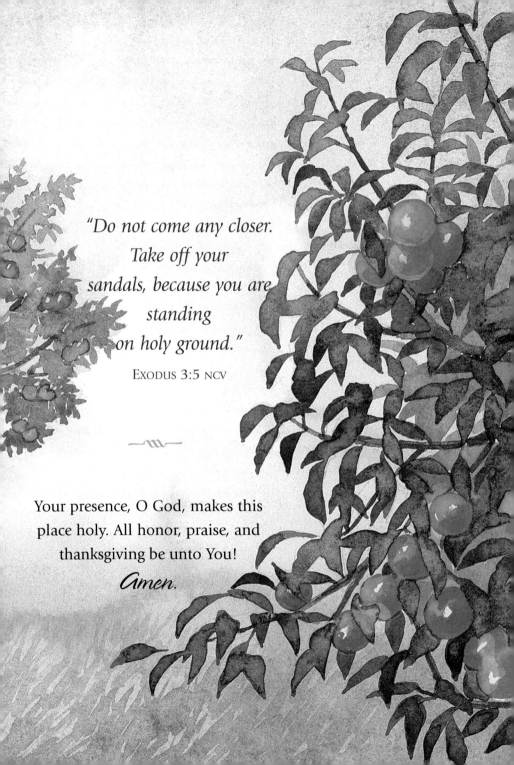

"Do not come any closer.
Take off your
sandals, because you are
standing
on holy ground."

EXODUS 3:5 NCV

Your presence, O God, makes this
place holy. All honor, praise, and
thanksgiving be unto You!
Amen.

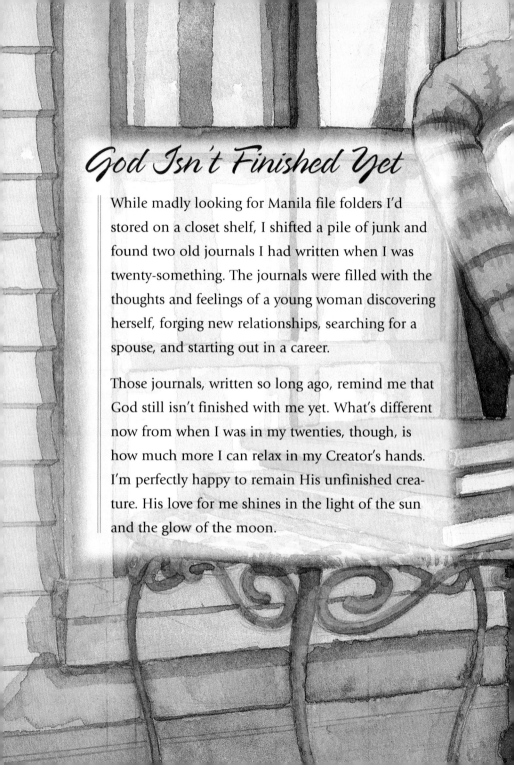

God Isn't Finished Yet

While madly looking for Manila file folders I'd stored on a closet shelf, I shifted a pile of junk and found two old journals I had written when I was twenty-something. The journals were filled with the thoughts and feelings of a young woman discovering herself, forging new relationships, searching for a spouse, and starting out in a career.

Those journals, written so long ago, remind me that God still isn't finished with me yet. What's different now from when I was in my twenties, though, is how much more I can relax in my Creator's hands. I'm perfectly happy to remain His unfinished creature. His love for me shines in the light of the sun and the glow of the moon.

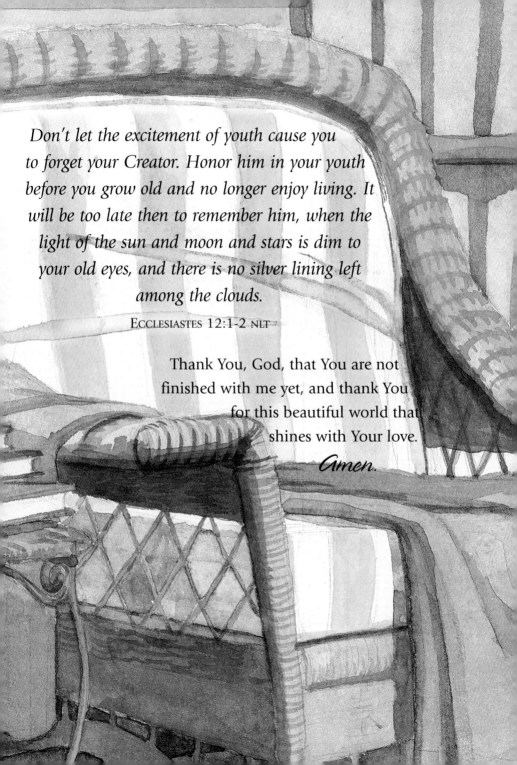

*Don't let the excitement of youth cause you
to forget your Creator. Honor him in your youth
before you grow old and no longer enjoy living. It
will be too late then to remember him, when the
light of the sun and moon and stars is dim to
your old eyes, and there is no silver lining left
among the clouds.*

ECCLESIASTES 12:1-2 NLT

Thank You, God, that You are not
finished with me yet, and thank You
for this beautiful world that
shines with Your love.
Amen.

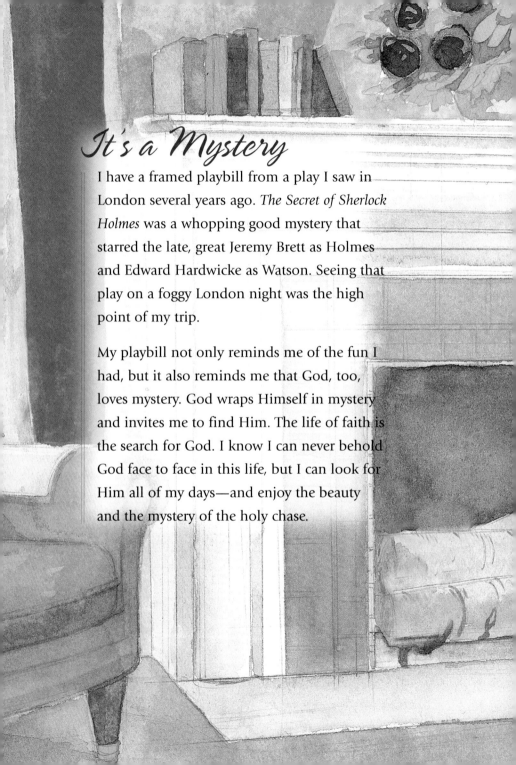

It's a Mystery

I have a framed playbill from a play I saw in London several years ago. *The Secret of Sherlock Holmes* was a whopping good mystery that starred the late, great Jeremy Brett as Holmes and Edward Hardwicke as Watson. Seeing that play on a foggy London night was the high point of my trip.

My playbill not only reminds me of the fun I had, but it also reminds me that God, too, loves mystery. God wraps Himself in mystery and invites me to find Him. The life of faith is the search for God. I know I can never behold God face to face in this life, but I can look for Him all of my days—and enjoy the beauty and the mystery of the holy chase.

We speak the wisdom of God in a mystery,
even the hidden wisdom, which God
ordained before the world unto our glory.

1 CORINTHIANS 2:7 KJV

O God, let me search after You with passion
and love all the days of my life.

Amen.

The Nightstand

I keep a small statue of a fat, pear-shaped cat on my nightstand. I bought it in a seaside boutique long ago. The statue reminds me of one of my cats, who is very pear-shaped when she sits down, and whom I love very much.

My little cat statue is a sign to me. It reminds me every morning that the reason I am on this planet is to love and that God will be with me when I love with my whole heart. It's easy for me to forget to be loving and, instead, to lapse into a state of taking life and those I love for granted. I need signs, like the little cat, to remind me how precious life is and how wise it is to spend my life with love.

Once these signs are fulfilled,
do whatever your hand finds
to do, for God is with you.

1 SAMUEL 10:7 NIV

—ɱ—

Lord, give me signs today that
help me to remember that You
want me to love You
and all those I meet.
Amen.

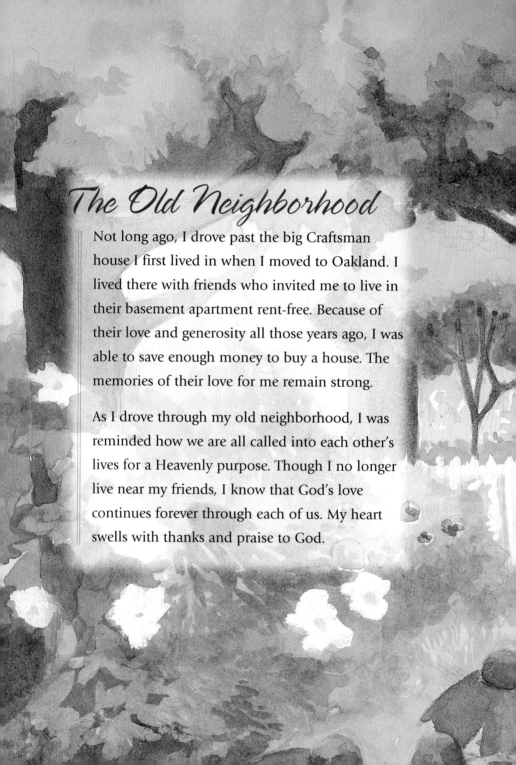

The Old Neighborhood

Not long ago, I drove past the big Craftsman house I first lived in when I moved to Oakland. I lived there with friends who invited me to live in their basement apartment rent-free. Because of their love and generosity all those years ago, I was able to save enough money to buy a house. The memories of their love for me remain strong.

As I drove through my old neighborhood, I was reminded how we are all called into each other's lives for a Heavenly purpose. Though I no longer live near my friends, I know that God's love continues forever through each of us. My heart swells with thanks and praise to God.

Thank the LORD
because he is good.
His love continues forever.

1 CHRONICLES 16:34 NCV

O God, You are good. Help
me to remember Your
goodness today in the lives
of all whom I touch.
Amen.

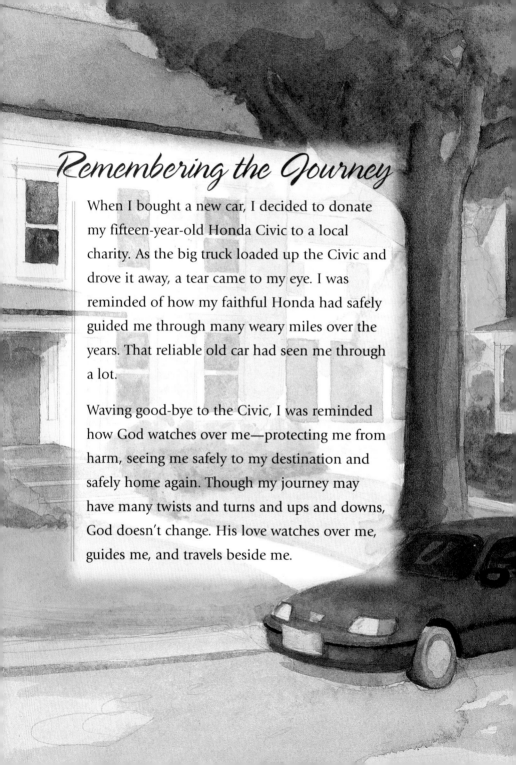

Remembering the Journey

When I bought a new car, I decided to donate my fifteen-year-old Honda Civic to a local charity. As the big truck loaded up the Civic and drove it away, a tear came to my eye. I was reminded of how my faithful Honda had safely guided me through many weary miles over the years. That reliable old car had seen me through a lot.

Waving good-bye to the Civic, I was reminded how God watches over me—protecting me from harm, seeing me safely to my destination and safely home again. Though my journey may have many twists and turns and ups and downs, God doesn't change. His love watches over me, guides me, and travels beside me.

*I have traveled many weary miles. I have
faced danger from flooded rivers and from
robbers. I have faced danger from my own
people, the Jews, as well as from the Gentiles.
I have faced dangers in the cities, in the
deserts, and on the stormy seas. And I have
faced danger from men who claim to be
Christians but are not.*

2 CORINTHIANS 11:26 NLT

Watch over me today, O God.
See me safely to my destination
and safely home again.

Amen.

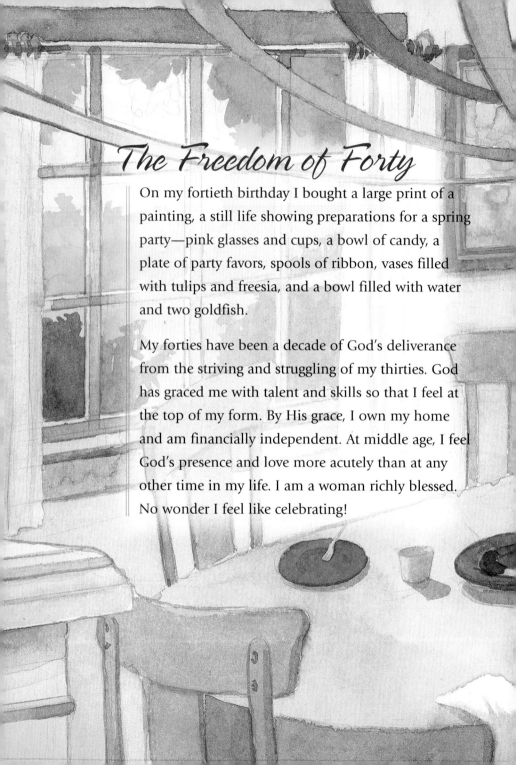

The Freedom of Forty

On my fortieth birthday I bought a large print of a painting, a still life showing preparations for a spring party—pink glasses and cups, a bowl of candy, a plate of party favors, spools of ribbon, vases filled with tulips and freesia, and a bowl filled with water and two goldfish.

My forties have been a decade of God's deliverance from the striving and struggling of my thirties. God has graced me with talent and skills so that I feel at the top of my form. By His grace, I own my home and am financially independent. At middle age, I feel God's presence and love more acutely than at any other time in my life. I am a woman richly blessed. No wonder I feel like celebrating!

I will walk around freely because I sought out your guiding principles.

PSALM 119:45 GOD'S WORD

⟶ ⟅ ⟵

For all the blessings of this life, O Lord, for the blessings I see, and the blessings I've yet to see, I rejoice to give You thanks.

Amen.

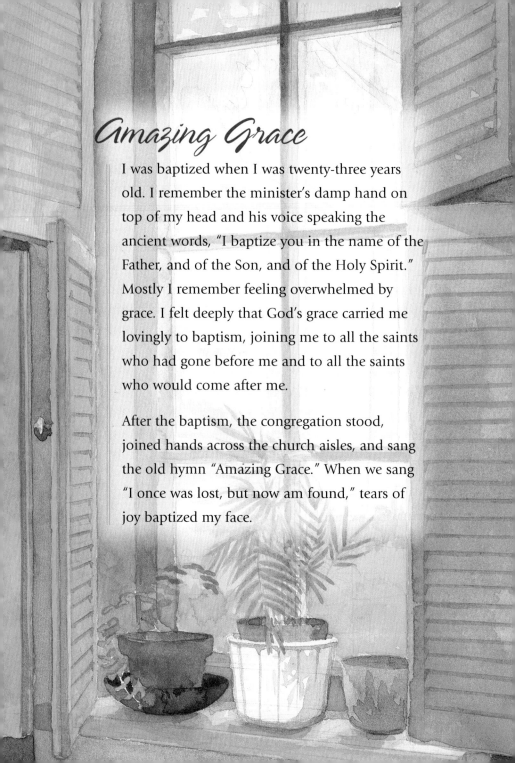

Amazing Grace

I was baptized when I was twenty-three years old. I remember the minister's damp hand on top of my head and his voice speaking the ancient words, "I baptize you in the name of the Father, and of the Son, and of the Holy Spirit." Mostly I remember feeling overwhelmed by grace. I felt deeply that God's grace carried me lovingly to baptism, joining me to all the saints who had gone before me and to all the saints who would come after me.

After the baptism, the congregation stood, joined hands across the church aisles, and sang the old hymn "Amazing Grace." When we sang "I once was lost, but now am found," tears of joy baptized my face.

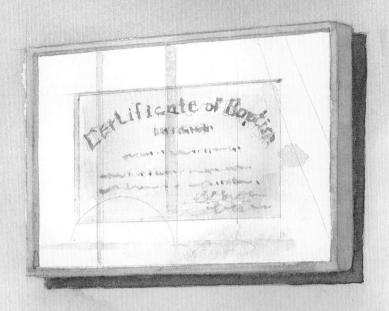

*Since we are justified by faith, we have peace
with God through our Lord Jesus Christ, through
whom we have obtained access to this grace in
which we stand; and we boast in our hope of
sharing the glory of God.*

ROMANS 5:1-2 NRSV

Let me be swept away by Your grace today, O Lord, and
join all of Your saints in the hope of glory.

Amen.

The Fence-Raising

A few years ago, I bought a 1953 ranch home. Unfortunately, the backyard fence also dated from 1953. Many slats were missing, and a large bush held up most of the fence. Two good friends who knew what they were doing generously offered to help me build me a new fence.

When the day came to start work on the fence, my friends assembled four of their friends to come help. It was like an old-fashioned barn-raising—except this was a fence-raising! The new fence is beautiful with arbors on top that support climbing roses and jasmine. When I look at my fence, I am reminded to be generous toward others, and so express my gratitude to God for His goodness.

You will be made rich in every way so that you can be generous on every occasion, and through us your generosity will result in thanksgiving to God. This service that you perform is not only supplying the needs of God's people but is also overflowing in many expressions of thanks to God.

2 CORINTHIANS 9:11-12 NIV

Help me to find ways to be generous toward others today, O God, that my thanksgiving may be pleasing in Your sight. *Amen.*

The Woodworker

My dad is a woodworker. Mostly he carves in wood, but he occasionally builds and refinishes furniture. A few years ago, Dad made for me a quilt rack out of solid oak. It is a beautiful, graceful thing. It is also strong—it holds several large, heavy quilts. My lovely, sturdy quilt rack reminds me of my father.

When I watch my father working on a piece of wood, I see a little bit of God. God's faithfulness toward me is far greater than my father's. God's faithfulness is tougher than oak, more solid than rock. I know I won't have Dad forever. But when I look at my quilt rack, I know that God will never leave me; His faithfulness will never fail.

There is no one holy like the L<small>ORD</small>,
Indeed, there is no one besides You, Nor
is there any rock like our God.

1 S<small>AMUEL</small> 2:2 <small>NASB</small>

O Lord, help me to rest in Your
faithfulness toward me. Let me know
Your eternal love today.

Amen.

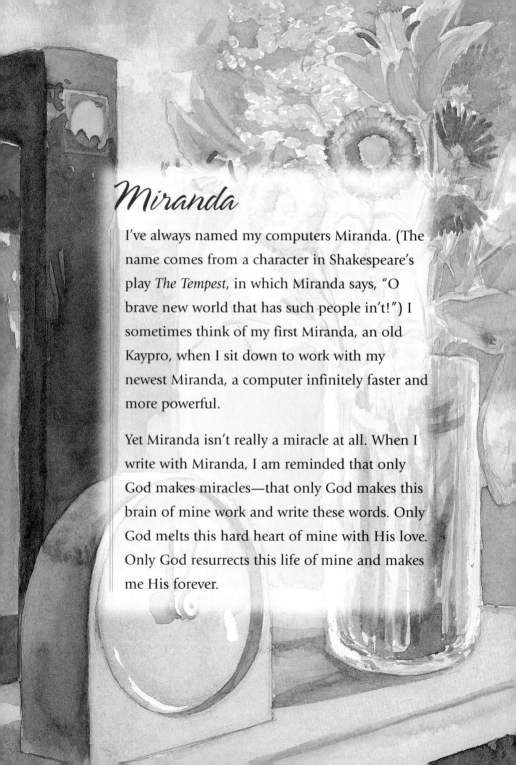

Miranda

I've always named my computers Miranda. (The
name comes from a character in Shakespeare's
play *The Tempest*, in which Miranda says, "O
brave new world that has such people in't!") I
sometimes think of my first Miranda, an old
Kaypro, when I sit down to work with my
newest Miranda, a computer infinitely faster and
more powerful.

Yet Miranda isn't really a miracle at all. When I
write with Miranda, I am reminded that only
God makes miracles—that only God makes this
brain of mine work and write these words. Only
God melts this hard heart of mine with His love.
Only God resurrects this life of mine and makes
me His forever.

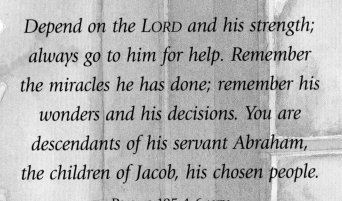

Depend on the LORD and his strength;
always go to him for help. Remember
the miracles he has done; remember his
wonders and his decisions. You are
descendants of his servant Abraham,
the children of Jacob, his chosen people.

PSALMS 105:4-6 NCV

I remember today
the wonderful things
You have done in my
life, O Lord. Thank
You for
Your miracles.
Amen.

The Legacy of Friendship

Photographs are memories in print. One of my favorite photos is more than fifteen years old and sits in a frame in my study. It's a picture of my best friend, Greg, and me. We are young and making goofy faces at the camera. Though Greg now lives three thousand miles away, we still talk once a week on the phone.

Friendship is memory clothed in another person. God sends us friends to help us remember how far we've come on our pilgrimage in Christ. Greg is one of the very few people outside my family who has watched God help me change and grow over the years. Thanks be to God, a friend is always a friend. I can count on Greg to keep traveling with me through life and faith.

*A friend always loves, and a
brother is born to share trouble.*

PROVERBS 17:17 GOD'S WORD

Thank You, O God, for friends who
tell me how much You love me.

Amen.

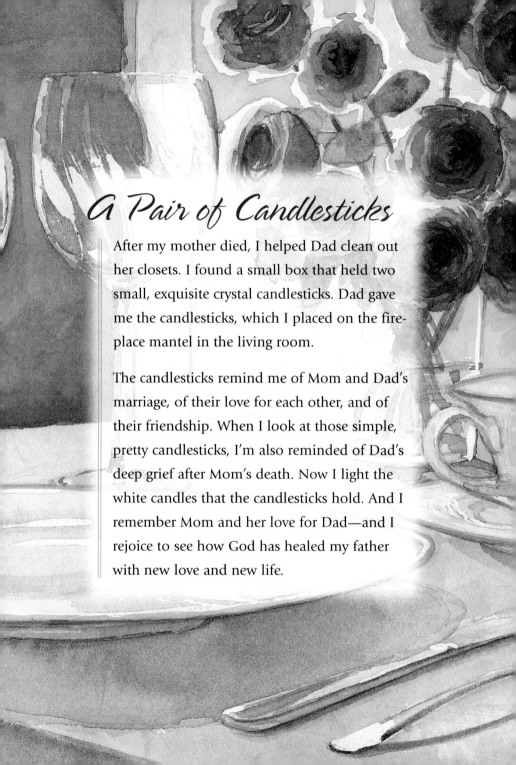

A Pair of Candlesticks

After my mother died, I helped Dad clean out her closets. I found a small box that held two small, exquisite crystal candlesticks. Dad gave me the candlesticks, which I placed on the fireplace mantel in the living room.

The candlesticks remind me of Mom and Dad's marriage, of their love for each other, and of their friendship. When I look at those simple, pretty candlesticks, I'm also reminded of Dad's deep grief after Mom's death. Now I light the white candles that the candlesticks hold. And I remember Mom and her love for Dad—and I rejoice to see how God has healed my father with new love and new life.

For you who revere my name the sun of righteousness shall rise, with healing in its wings. You shall go out leaping like calves from the stall.

MALACHI 4:2 NRSV

O God, You light up the darkness
with Your healing love, and I rejoice
to give You thanks.

Amen.

Back to the Future

Several years ago I framed a passage from *Charlotte's Web* by E. B. White. In the passage, Charlotte the spider tells Albert the pig that winter will one day pass and that spring will make the world beautiful again. The world was a pretty cold, dark place for me when I framed that passage. I wasn't sure spring would ever come again, but by God's grace it did.

Sometimes I have to remember the past in order to travel into the uncertain future. I read those words from the past occasionally to remind me that only God lasts forever. All other things change, like the seasons. Wintry times can't last because God's words of mercy and grace will eventually bring a springtime of hope and healing.

"He whom God has sent speaks the words of God; for He gives the Spirit without measure."

JOHN 3:34 NASB

O God, change my world into springtime with Your words of love and grace.

Amen.

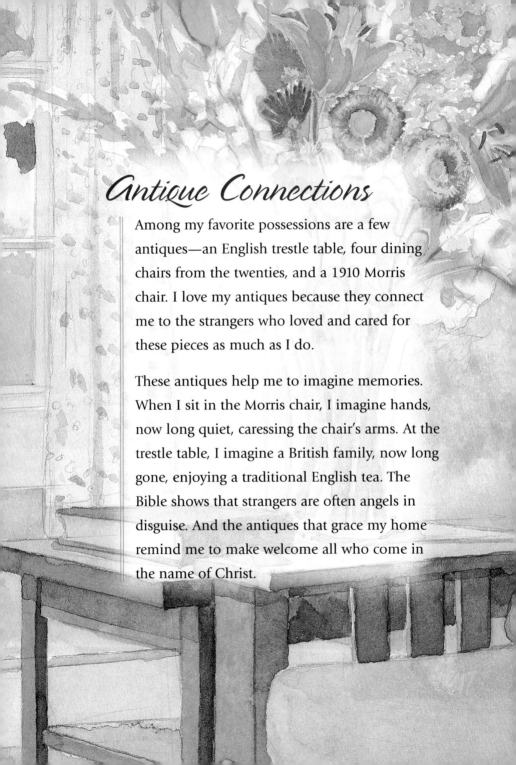

Antique Connections

Among my favorite possessions are a few antiques—an English trestle table, four dining chairs from the twenties, and a 1910 Morris chair. I love my antiques because they connect me to the strangers who loved and cared for these pieces as much as I do.

These antiques help me to imagine memories. When I sit in the Morris chair, I imagine hands, now long quiet, caressing the chair's arms. At the trestle table, I imagine a British family, now long gone, enjoying a traditional English tea. The Bible shows that strangers are often angels in disguise. And the antiques that grace my home remind me to make welcome all who come in the name of Christ.

Don't forget to show hospitality to strangers, for some who have done this have entertained angels without realizing it!

HEBREWS 13:2 NLT

———

Lord, help me to make strangers
as welcome as angels today.
Amen.

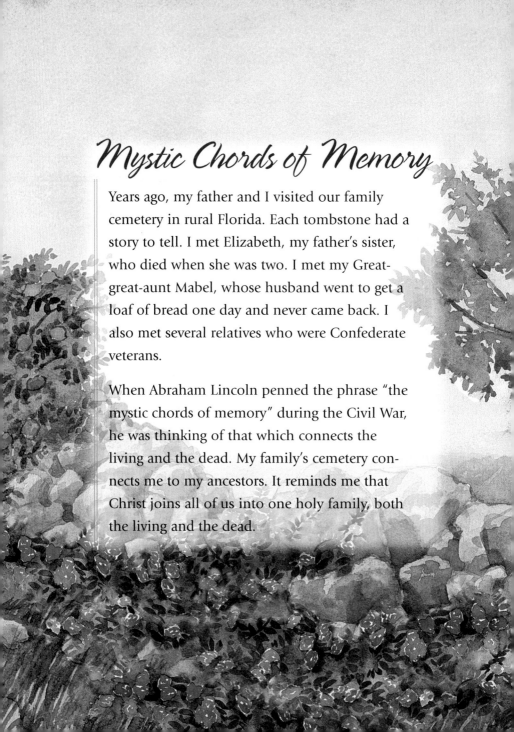

Mystic Chords of Memory

Years ago, my father and I visited our family cemetery in rural Florida. Each tombstone had a story to tell. I met Elizabeth, my father's sister, who died when she was two. I met my Great-great-aunt Mabel, whose husband went to get a loaf of bread one day and never came back. I also met several relatives who were Confederate veterans.

When Abraham Lincoln penned the phrase "the mystic chords of memory" during the Civil War, he was thinking of that which connects the living and the dead. My family's cemetery connects me to my ancestors. It reminds me that Christ joins all of us into one holy family, both the living and the dead.

*In bringing many sons to glory, it was
fitting that God, for whom and through
whom everything exists,
should make the author
of their salvation perfect
through suffering. Both the
one who makes men holy
and those who are made holy
are of the same family. So Jesus is
not ashamed to call them brothers.*

HEBREWS 2:10-11 NIV

Nothing can separate me, O God, from those
who have gone to glory, for we are bound
together in Your love.

Amen.

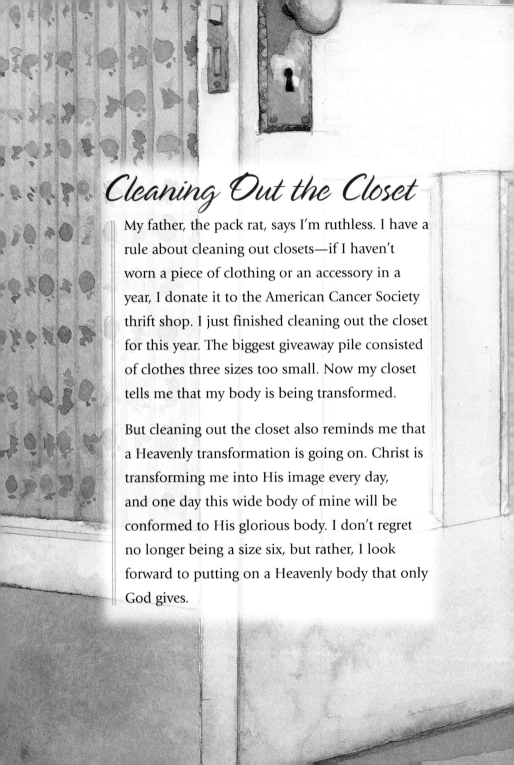

Cleaning Out the Closet

My father, the pack rat, says I'm ruthless. I have a rule about cleaning out closets—if I haven't worn a piece of clothing or an accessory in a year, I donate it to the American Cancer Society thrift shop. I just finished cleaning out the closet for this year. The biggest giveaway pile consisted of clothes three sizes too small. Now my closet tells me that my body is being transformed.

But cleaning out the closet also reminds me that a Heavenly transformation is going on. Christ is transforming me into His image every day, and one day this wide body of mine will be conformed to His glorious body. I don't regret no longer being a size six, but rather, I look forward to putting on a Heavenly body that only God gives.

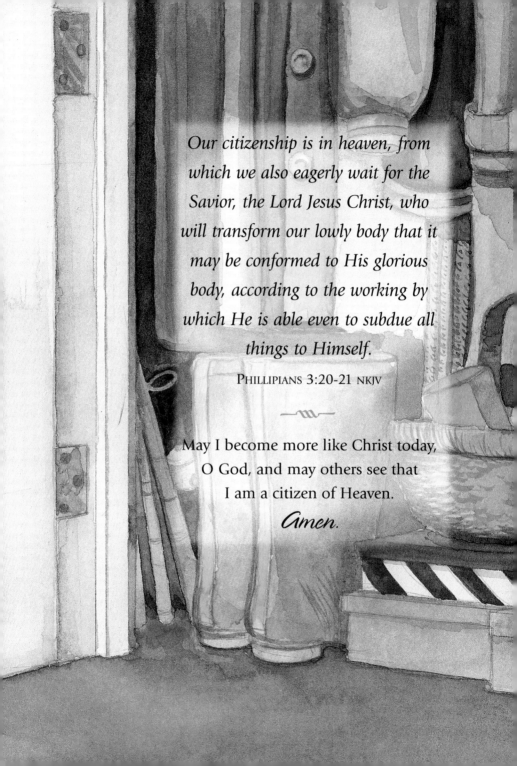

Our citizenship is in heaven, from which we also eagerly wait for the Savior, the Lord Jesus Christ, who will transform our lowly body that it may be conformed to His glorious body, according to the working by which He is able even to subdue all things to Himself.

PHILLIPIANS 3:20-21 NKJV

—⁓—

May I become more like Christ today,
O God, and may others see that
I am a citizen of Heaven.
Amen.

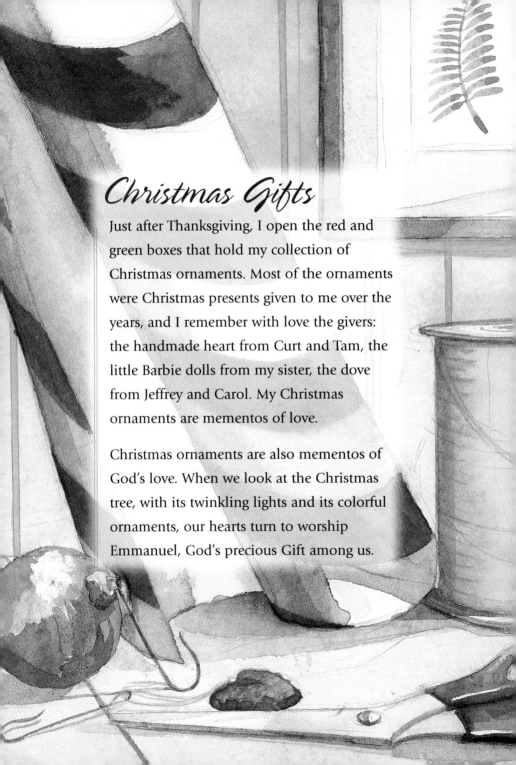

Christmas Gifts

Just after Thanksgiving, I open the red and green boxes that hold my collection of Christmas ornaments. Most of the ornaments were Christmas presents given to me over the years, and I remember with love the givers: the handmade heart from Curt and Tam, the little Barbie dolls from my sister, the dove from Jeffrey and Carol. My Christmas ornaments are mementos of love.

Christmas ornaments are also mementos of God's love. When we look at the Christmas tree, with its twinkling lights and its colorful ornaments, our hearts turn to worship Emmanuel, God's precious Gift among us.

People everywhere will remember and will turn to the L{ord}. All the families of the nations will worship him.

P{salm} 22:27 {ncv}

Let me discover today, O Lord,
a memento of Your love and
presence with me.

Amen.

Knit One, Purl Two

When I first learned to knit about twelve years ago, I went at it like a fiend—I knitted fourteen sweaters in one year. Every time I reach into my cedar chest to pull out one of those sweaters, I'm reminded of what I liked most about knitting—it is relaxing and tranquil. When I knit, my hands are kept busy while my heart is free to daydream about God.

Someone once said that we are most like God when we create. When I make things—a sweater, a cake, a book—I feel closer to God. It's as though God, the Creator, loves for me to imitate Him. When I do, my spirit is renewed and refreshed, and my heart sings my Creator's praises.

Create in me a clean heart, O God;
and renew a right spirit within me.

PSALM 51:10 KJV

May the work of my hands please You,
O God, to give me a clean heart
and a renewed spirit.

Amen.

Cans of Paint

I must have twenty different cans of latex paint in my garage. I've been slowly repainting eight rooms in my house since I bought the place three years ago. I'm doing all the work myself. Seeing all those cans of paint reminds me of how hard I've worked on my house: new landscaping in the front and back, a remodeled kitchen and bath, new hardwood floors, a new fence, and new windows.

But it's been worth all the work—and money! The sweat equity I put into my house has made it a place of welcome, comfort, and love. It is a place where God and I can dwell in peace.

I will make Your name to be remembered in all generations; Therefore the people shall praise You forever and ever.

PSALM 45:17 NKJV

O Lord, may all who dwell in my house remember and praise You forever!

Amen.

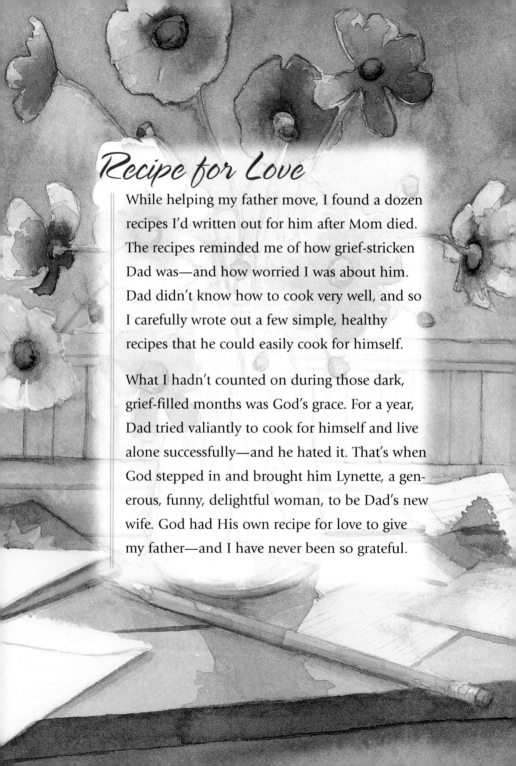

Recipe for Love

While helping my father move, I found a dozen recipes I'd written out for him after Mom died. The recipes reminded me of how grief-stricken Dad was—and how worried I was about him. Dad didn't know how to cook very well, and so I carefully wrote out a few simple, healthy recipes that he could easily cook for himself.

What I hadn't counted on during those dark, grief-filled months was God's grace. For a year, Dad tried valiantly to cook for himself and live alone successfully—and he hated it. That's when God stepped in and brought him Lynette, a generous, funny, delightful woman, to be Dad's new wife. God had His own recipe for love to give my father—and I have never been so grateful.

You have turned my mourning into dancing; you have taken off my sackcloth and clothed me with joy, so that my soul may praise you and not be silent. O LORD my God, I will give thanks to you forever.

PSALMS 30:11-12 NRSV

You make my soul glad, O Lord, and I will not be silent, but will sing Your praises.

Amen.

Powerful Place Settings

Every time I set my table with my yellow-rimmed bistro plates, I'm reminded of the power of faith. Several years ago, I bought my first house. I went deeply into debt to do it, and I was barely making ends meet.

My friend Liz gave me four place settings of the yellow bistro-ware as a housewarming gift. She gave me a much greater gift than pretty plates, however. She gave me her prayers. She had faith in God's power to provide for me when I did not. She carried me in prayer when I was too afraid to pray. During that first year of home ownership, God did take care of me and meet all of my needs. And He did so, largely because of Liz, who faithfully fulfilled the law of love.

Carry each other's burdens, and in this way you will fulfill the law of Christ.

GALATIANS 6:2 NIV

O Lord, help me to be strong and carry another's burdens, if need be. All for the love of You.

Amen.

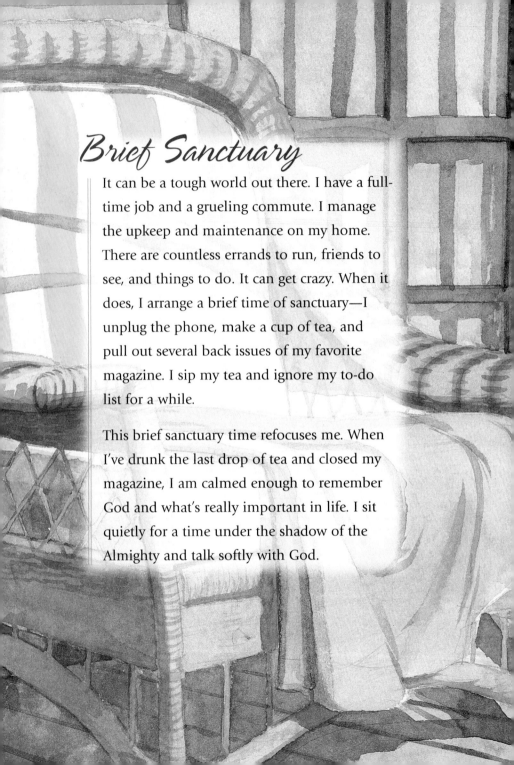

Brief Sanctuary

It can be a tough world out there. I have a full-time job and a grueling commute. I manage the upkeep and maintenance on my home. There are countless errands to run, friends to see, and things to do. It can get crazy. When it does, I arrange a brief time of sanctuary—I unplug the phone, make a cup of tea, and pull out several back issues of my favorite magazine. I sip my tea and ignore my to-do list for a while.

This brief sanctuary time refocuses me. When I've drunk the last drop of tea and closed my magazine, I am calmed enough to remember God and what's really important in life. I sit quietly for a time under the shadow of the Almighty and talk softly with God.

You who live in the shelter of the Most High, who abide in the shadow of the Almighty, will say to the LORD, "My refuge and my fortress; my God, in whom I trust."

PSALMS 91:1-2 NRSV

Give me time for sanctuary today, O God, so I can refocus and spend time with You.

Amen.

The Scent of Memory

Mock-orange trees line many of the streets of Berkeley, California, and in spring and summer the scent of their blossoms fills the air. For me, that scent always triggers wonderful memories of first love. Tom was my first college love—a dear, wonderful young man. At about the same time I met him, I also met God. The scent of the mock-orange blossoms reminds me of walking down Channing Way to church each Sunday, my heart so full of love for God that I thought I would burst. Tom has been gone a long time now, but God's love is always with me.

I planted two mock-orange trees in my front yard. The scent of their blossoms fills me with wonder and delight at the awesome power of God's perfect love.

There is no fear in love; but perfect love casteth out fear: because fear hath torment. He that feareth is not made perfect in love. We love him, because he first loved us.

1 JOHN 4:18-19 KJV

O God, You are my first love
and my last, and I rejoice
in Your perfect love for me.
Amen.

History

Many of the books in my study are about American history. My history books help me remember who we Americans are and how we got to where we are today as a people.

In the Bible, God's people enjoyed love and care, but they also continually needed His forgiveness and mercy. The same is true for America. American history reminds me that I need to be grateful to God for all that is good about our nation and all that I enjoy. I also need God's forgiveness to heal my country from the parts of its past of which I am not so proud. When I read my history books, I remember to pray for my country, to ask for God's mercy, and to seek the wisdom needed to always do what's good and right.

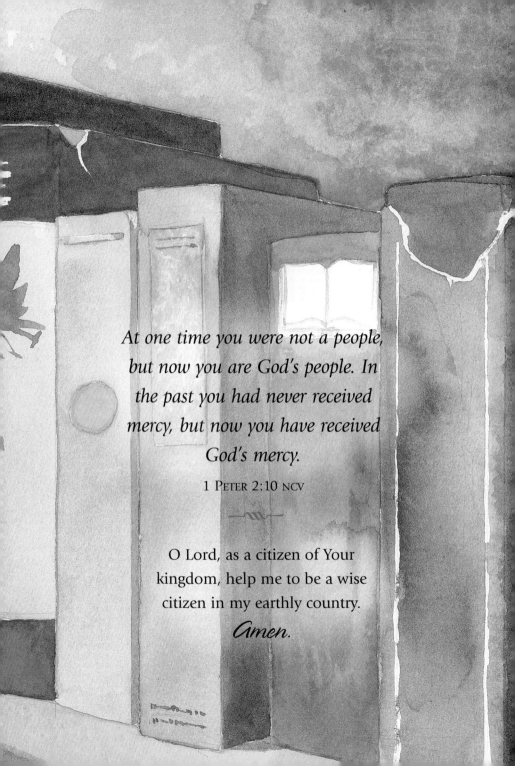

At one time you were not a people,
but now you are God's people. In
the past you had never received
mercy, but now you have received
God's mercy.

1 PETER 2:10 NCV

O Lord, as a citizen of Your
kingdom, help me to be a wise
citizen in my earthly country.

Amen.

Reunion

One of my best friends from college paid me a visit recently. We sat by the fire, drank many cups of tea, and talked for hours. We reminisced about our college days and our friends. We talked about ourselves and about how God had worked in our lives over the years. Joanne told me of the joys of raising a family and of her painful divorce after twenty-three years of marriage.

My reunion with her reminded me of God's timing. No matter how carefully we plan our days, our lives, God has His own timing for us. Joanne said to me: "I'm ready to trust God's timing in all of this and to look for Christ's love in the eyes of friends and family."

"Always be ready! You don't know when the Son of Man will come."

MATTHEW 24:44 CEV

O God, sometimes I don't understand Your timing for my life—but I'm ready to look for You in the eyes of those I love.

Amen.

The First House

A while ago, I drove by the first home I bought, and I was reminded of my horrible case of buyer's remorse. California was in the middle of a devastating economic recession, but the low prices for houses allowed me to afford one— barely. So I took the plunge. Not long after I bought my house, home prices plunged even further, and newspapers were full of stories about people fleeing hard times in California. I began to think I'd made a horrible mistake.

My case of buyer's remorse taught me that the life of faith means living for the long term. It means trusting that God is in control and that goodness and mercy will one day prevail.

The love of Christ controls us, having concluded this, that one died for all, therefore all died; and He died for all, so that they who live might no longer live for themselves, but for Him who died and rose again on their behalf.

2 CORINTHIANS 5:14-15 NASB

O Lord, You are in control of my life today, tomorrow, and always. Help me to take a long-term perspective of Your love today.

Amen.

The Bible

I bought my first Bible when I was twenty-three and just beginning to live the life of faith. I still have it and keep it in a place of honor in my study. It is a tattered thing. The cloth binding has worn away, exposing the cardboard on the cover's corners. The edges of the pages are dirty and well thumbed. Inside, the print on the pages is heavily marked with a yellow highlighter, and there are copious notes in most of the margins.

There have been many other Bibles over the years—but that first Bible of mine was a portal to God's grace. When I thumb through my old Bible today, God still greets me through its pages. I am carried by His grace once again through Heaven's bright gates.

The LORD God is a sun and shield; The LORD will give grace and glory; No good thing will he withhold From those who walk uprightly.

PSALM 84:11 NKJV

O God, let me find healing and forgiveness in Your words today. *Amen.*

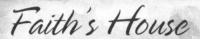

Faith's House

I once had an unforgettable friend named Faith.
She owned a rambling old Craftsman-style
home filled with comfortable furniture, well-
worn antiques, and lots and lots of books. But
the best part of Faith's house was its big kitchen.
Cluttered and filled with light, it was always
ready for friends. It was also filled with angels.

When Faith prayed, God listened. Faith's prayers
were always strong, powerful, and confident and
were sustained by her rock-solid faith. When she
prayed, I could hear the rush of angels' wings fill
the kitchen's corners and rafters. To this day,
whenever I remember Faith and her prayer-filled
kitchen, I hear afar off the sound of angels' wings.

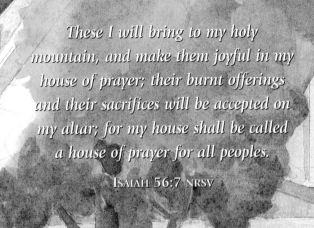

*These I will bring to my holy
mountain, and make them joyful in my
house of prayer; their burnt offerings
and their sacrifices will be accepted on
my altar; for my house shall be called
a house of prayer for all peoples.*

Isaiah 56:7 nrsv

May my prayers come before
You, O God, as sweet incense,
that You may be well pleased.
Amen.

Term Papers

While looking for something else, I stumbled across a big, thick binder stuffed with all my old term papers from college. I gave up my search and sat down to read some of them. Oh, the tortured prose!

I hated to write when I was in college. Needless to say, I had no intention of becoming a professional writer. But, God had other plans. As I look back over my life, I see that God almost always has had different plans for me than what I had in mind. I now see that the life of faith is one of surrender—of giving up to God and letting Him have His way. Any plans I make today must be flexible enough to let me follow where God leads.

The steps of the godly are
directed by the LORD. He delights in
every detail of their lives.

PSALM 37:23 NLT

—⁓—

Direct my steps today, O Lord, that I might
bring honor and glory to You.
Amen.

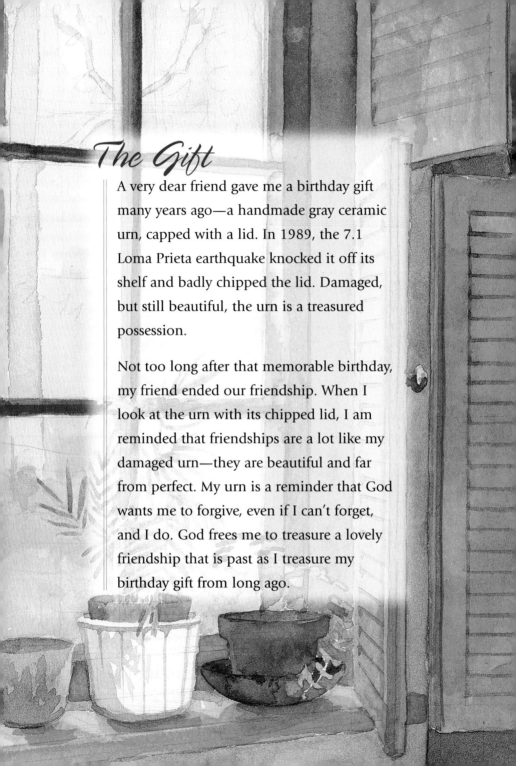

The Gift

A very dear friend gave me a birthday gift many years ago—a handmade gray ceramic urn, capped with a lid. In 1989, the 7.1 Loma Prieta earthquake knocked it off its shelf and badly chipped the lid. Damaged, but still beautiful, the urn is a treasured possession.

Not too long after that memorable birthday, my friend ended our friendship. When I look at the urn with its chipped lid, I am reminded that friendships are a lot like my damaged urn—they are beautiful and far from perfect. My urn is a reminder that God wants me to forgive, even if I can't forget, and I do. God frees me to treasure a lovely friendship that is past as I treasure my birthday gift from long ago.

"If you forgive others for their transgressions, your heavenly Father will also forgive you."

MATTHEW 6:14 NASB

—∽—

Help me to forgive others, O Lord, so that I can become free to enjoy them again.

Amen.

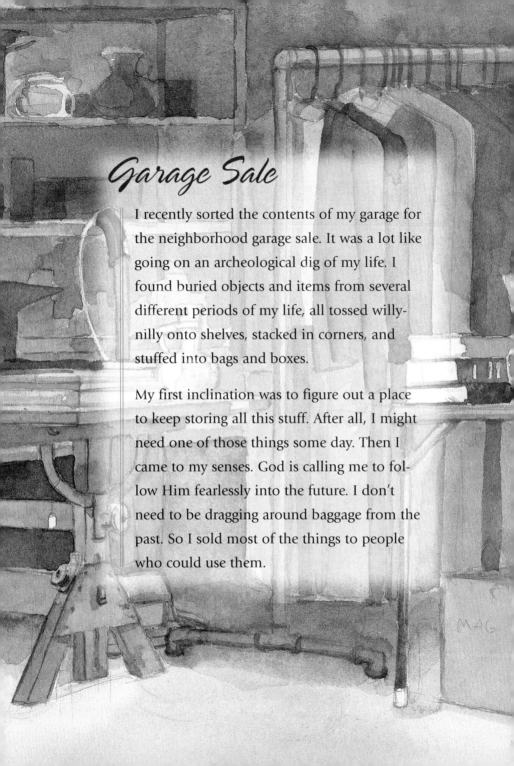

Garage Sale

I recently sorted the contents of my garage for the neighborhood garage sale. It was a lot like going on an archeological dig of my life. I found buried objects and items from several different periods of my life, all tossed willy-nilly onto shelves, stacked in corners, and stuffed into bags and boxes.

My first inclination was to figure out a place to keep storing all this stuff. After all, I might need one of those things some day. Then I came to my senses. God is calling me to follow Him fearlessly into the future. I don't need to be dragging around baggage from the past. So I sold most of the things to people who could use them.

There is surely a future
hope for you, and your
hope will not be cut off.

PROVERBS 23:18 NIV

Lord, help me to get rid
of the things that keep
me from following You
where You lead.
Amen.

Trust God

I used to like working at the bank. It was a good, interesting job, and the bank's CEO was providing great leadership, management, and direction. I planned to work there until I retired. Then another big bank acquired our bank. Not long afterward, our CEO sent a letter to employees asking us to "trust the vision, trust each other, and trust the possibilities" of the acquisition. We trusted him, and thousands of people lost their jobs (including the CEO).

I keep a framed copy of the CEO's letter in my study to remind me whom to trust. My experience at the bank taught me to trust in God and God alone.

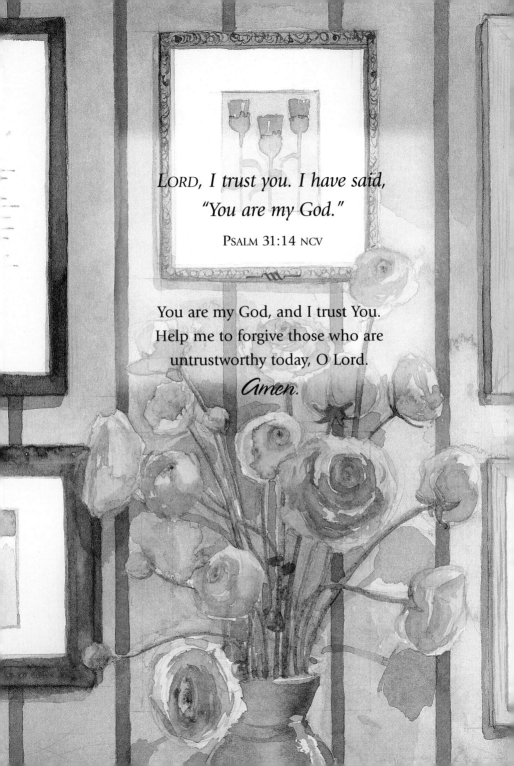

LORD, *I trust you. I have said,*
"You are my God."

PSALM 31:14 NCV

You are my God, and I trust You.
Help me to forgive those who are
untrustworthy today, O Lord.
Amen.

The Time Capsule

My house is a year older than I am. It is a split-level ranch style, typical for mid-twentieth-century houses in California. It was a custom-built luxury home. My home is a silent time capsule.

Now, I'm adding my own memories to this time capsule of mine. Since I moved in, I've been hard at work giving the house a needed face-lift. The house is slowly showing me how it must have looked in its glory days. As my home and I age gracefully into this new century, God fills my house with His goodness and the warmth of His love. Family and friends help me add more memories into my time capsule that will one day declare the glory of God's love to a new generation.

We know that all things work together for good for those who love God, who are called according to his purpose.

ROMANS 8:28 NRSV

O God, fill my home today with Your goodness, love, and the warmth of Your presence. *Amen.*

The Street

I try not to take my street for granted. If it weren't for living on my street, I might never have met Greg and Pam, a married couple who have become my friends as well as my neighbors. Greg is an economist, and Pam is a successful artist. Both work out of their home. I love to tour Pam's studio and look at her latest sculptures. I enjoy talking with Greg about his writing and research.

God loves neighborhoods because neighborhoods are like extended families that join us to others. God rejoices to see all of us living and working together in harmony to make His world a more beautiful place.

May God Almighty bless you,
And make you fruitful and
multiply you, That you may be
an assembly of peoples.

GENESIS 28:3 NKJV

O God, bless my neighbors. Help
us to live together in a way that
brings glory to You.
Amen.

A Garden

One of my favorite hobbies is gardening. I have a flower garden where the front lawn used to be, and I have a kitchen garden in the backyard. My gardens change and grow each year. In my kitchen garden, I may grow herbs one year and corn and tomatoes the next. Out front, I'm constantly transplanting—putting in new beds and pulling up old ones.

My gardens remind me that God is constantly creating and re-creating, making all things new. When I'm out working in my garden, I think of the Creator tending the world, making it beautiful and fruitful. In the winter, when it's too cold to be out, I look at my garden and am reminded that God never sleeps. He is constantly at work showing forth His glory in all of creation.

Hast thou not known? hast thou not heard, that *the everlasting* God, *the* LORD, *the Creator of the ends of the earth, fainteth not, neither is weary?* there is *no searching of his understanding. He giveth power to the faint; and to* them that have *no might he increaseth strength.*

ISAIAH 40:28-29 KJV

—⁓—

O God, You are creating a beautiful world. Help me to slow down today and enjoy it.

Amen.

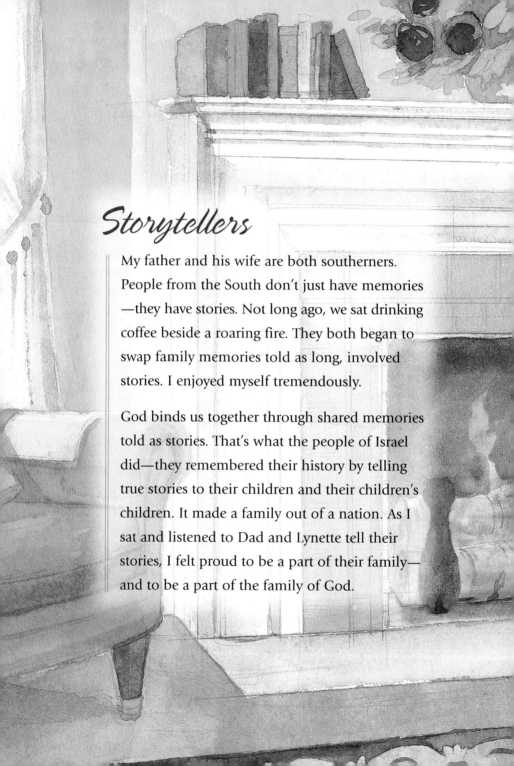

Storytellers

My father and his wife are both southerners. People from the South don't just have memories —they have stories. Not long ago, we sat drinking coffee beside a roaring fire. They both began to swap family memories told as long, involved stories. I enjoyed myself tremendously.

God binds us together through shared memories told as stories. That's what the people of Israel did—they remembered their history by telling true stories to their children and their children's children. It made a family out of a nation. As I sat and listened to Dad and Lynette tell their stories, I felt proud to be a part of their family— and to be a part of the family of God.

Tell your children about it,
Let your children tell their
children, And their children
another generation.

JOEL 1:3 NKJV

O God, do not let me forget
to tell my children the stories of
Your people, our family.
Amen.

God Remembers Us

I get very busy on weekends doing chores and running errands. I try to keep everything I need to do in my head, but it's just too much. I make lists, and then I forget where I put them.

There's a string tied around my finger right now. I forget now what it's supposed to remind me to do, but it does remind me that God never forgets. It is impossible for God to ever forget me or forsake me because I am His child. God's love and mercy, as vast as space, is as close as my next breath. It is not important that I get everything done today. It is only important to remember that God loves me and that He holds me in the palm of His hand.

"Can a mother forget her nursing child? Can she feel no love for a child she has borne? But even if that were possible, I would not forget you!"

ISAIAH 49:15 NLT

O God, as I go about my busy day today, help me to remember that I am Your precious child. *Amen.*